Simple Tax

Denice Houslin

This fourth edition is published by Sunesis Ministries Ltd. For more information about Sunesis Ministries Ltd, please visit:

www.stuartpattico.com

ISBN: 978-0-9956837-1-6

Acknowledgments

For my husband, my greatest supporter.

Table of Contents

Introduction

In 2010, when I first started working for myself, I thought Tax and Accounts would be simple.

I had my Maths GCSE. I knew I needed to charge for services I supplied, calculate how much I spent on travelling, stationery and my mobile phone, subtract that from what I had charged and then pay tax on the rest........simple!

Well maybe not.

I didn't, and still don't, see why I needed an accountant to calculate my income, subtract what I have spent and calculate a % for tax on the rest.

My accounts were not that complicated were they? Surely everything I needed to know could be found out from Her Majesty's Revenue and Customs (HMRC) website...right?

Well yes, but why did it take so long to understand what they were saying and what it all actually meant?

What about other things like, student loan repayments, advance payments and capital allowances?

Why were there different methods for calculating my travel costs?

Why are some clothes a business expense, but not others, and let's not even mention business lunches!

Hmmm.....this piece of string is not just long but very very long, how could I make it shorter?

That really was the beginning of my quest to make tax simple for the people like you and I, the Jo Bloggs with his or her own business that isn't really that complicated and who want an uncomplicated way of understanding tax, without paying through the nose for an accountant to add, subtract and calculate the odd percentage.

This guide is not written for the Limited company or the PLC, it's written for people like you and I who work for ourselves in a simple business, where we charge for what we do, pay for what we need and want to understand in a straightforward way how to work out how much tax we need to pay on the rest.

It's written for people who know how to add, subtract and work out the odd percentage and who don't necessarily want to pay someone £200+ every year out of their hard earned cash to do it for them.

You don't even have to know how to use Microsoft Excel, a notebook and a calculator will do, although personally I love spreadsheets as, if you know how to do a few simple formulas on them, then they add it all up for you as you go along.

If you want to understand tax in a simple way then it's really as straightforward as this – you make some money, you spend some of the money on things that HMRC sees as valid business expenses, and you pay tax on what is left.

But what about, as I'm often asked, the dreaded Self Assessment and the fines for late submission?

Well, in my opinion you have 3 options;

1. Complete the paper version and get it to HMRC by the 31/10 so they can work out your tax for you, although for most newly registering businesses the paper version is no longer an option.

2. Complete it online by 31st January and the online form will tell you how much tax you have to pay (although of course if you put the principles of this book into practice you will already be ahead of the game and know exactly how much tax you owe when the clock strikes midnight on the 5th April and the new tax year begins on the 6th!).

3. Give someone your 'simple' accounts and get them to do it for you, which should still be a lot cheaper than getting them to do your accounts from scratch.

If you want to choose option 1 or 2 then the section on Self Assessment will give you a good idea of how to go about it.

Whichever self assessment option you choose it's still going to be a lot cheaper than paying £200+ a year to your accountant to do it all for you from scratch.

If after reading this you are still not convinced this book can save you some money, I've even thrown in a few handy hints on the dreaded VAT that could possibly bring you in some additional money for virtually no effort.

You may find that voluntarily registering for VAT may bring you in some extra money that you can use to pay the accountant, if you still decided to use one, without putting a dent in your hard earned profit!

As you read through each chapter of this book my aim is always to explain each section in plain English so that, by the end of it, you have enough information to enable you to spend less time worrying about tax and accounts and more time building and delivering your amazing business.

Section 1: The Basics

Let's start at the beginning.

When you decide to work for yourself you need to tell HMRC as soon as possible and at least by the October of the second tax year that you are self-employed.

There are various ways you can work:

You can be an employee for a company some of the time and still be self employed in your own self employed business as well.

You can work in your own self employed business as well as working with someone else in another self employed business that is a 'partnership'.

You can be completely self employed as a sole trader.

There are many combinations and to be honest, HMRC don't really care how many 'jobs' you have. Their only interest is how much money you have made in total for each job or role that you have, how much you spent on allowable expenses, how much tax has already been deducted by say an employer, and how much tax you owe on the rest.

Naming your business

Your business name can just be your own name, or you can be a 'Trading as'. Trading as means an individual person who is trading as a business name. E.g. Jo Bloggs T/A Bloggs Painting and Decorating Services.

If you are 'Trading as' you cannot use things like PLC or Ltd after your company name. You are a sole trader. Sole traders have less complicated accounting requirements than Limited companies or Public Limited Companies.

As a Sole Trader you must include both your name and your trading as name on all your official paperwork.

You can also trade as a partnership. 'Ordinary Partnerships' are trading as businesses with more than one 'owner'. Limited liability partnerships (LLP's) are similar but there are restrictions on how much the partners can be made responsible for business debts. LLP partnerships also have some responsibilities regarding filing accounting information at Companies House.

If you are going into business with someone else it's always a good idea to get some advice from a tax professional about what type of partnership would be best for you and draw up a partnership agreement detailing who will do what and when and how the profits (or losses) will be split.

A Limited Company (Ltd) is an incorporated format which a business can set-up as, however as this guide is geared towards the one or two person business, who wants to keep it simple; it will not be covered here.

The Tax Year

The Tax year starts on the 6th April every year and ends on the 5th April the following year. Even if you start your new business on the 4th August in one year, you may find it easier to end that financial year on the 5th of April the following year so that you line up nicely with HMRC for all subsequent years.

Once the tax year ends on the 5th April you will have until the 31st January the following year to submit your self assessment and pay the tax due for that year.

You don't have to wait until the 31st January to file your self assessment; you can file it at any time once the tax year has ended.

On the 31st of January you may also need to pay an 'advance payment' for tax due for the tax year you are in which is due the following January. You will need to make a further advance payment on the 31st July. Advance payments are dependent on your income. If your tax bill for the year that has just ended is less than £1000 you will not have to pay advance payments.

Example

Year 1 of self employment ends 5th April 2017

You pay all tax owed for Year 1 on 31st January 2018 (you can pay it before this date if you want to)

On 31st January 18 you also pay an advance payment for the tax year that ends on 5th April 2018 (Year 2)

On 31st July 18 you pay a second advance payment for the tax owed for Year 2.

On 31st January 19 you pay the balance of your tax for Year 2 + an advance payment for the tax year that ends on 5th April 2019 (Year 3).....and so on.

Advance payments are always approximately 50% of the previous year's tax. So if your tax bill is £5000 in year 1 your advance payments for Year 2 will be two payments in January and July of £2500.

Many people will wait until January 29th and then spend the next 48 hours trawling through a carrier bag of receipts, trying to find the lost copy of that invoice they know they issued in November with gradually increasing anxiety as the £100 fine for late filing looms nearer.

A less stressful method is to, around the end of April/May, take a leisurely look at your well organised receipts and invoices, follow a step by step guide on how to complete your self assessment, pat yourself on the back of having put aside at least 20% of your earnings each month ready to pay your tax bill, sit back and relax, or continue on with your quest to increase your income this year with your brand new marketing idea.

Keeping on top of your tax bill

My single biggest tip on the basics of self employment is to be disciplined about your income right from the very beginning. Be your own 'employer'. Put a percentage of your income aside for tax, in a separate account, from the first month you become self employed. That way you will always be on top of your tax responsibilities and advance payments won't scare you!

Example

You become self employed on 6th April 2017. The tax year will end on the 5th April 2018. Any tax due needs to be paid by 31st January 2019, along with your first advance payment for the following year.

Every month you earn £2000. You decide to put aside 20% = £400 per month.

On the 5th April 2018 you have put away 12 payments = £4800.

You continue to do the same for the new tax year starting 6th April 2018. By January 2018, when your first tax payment is due, you have £8800 saved for tax (Year 1 = £4800 + Year 2 = £4000).

After expenses and tax allowances you find out you only need to pay £3500 for tax and student loan and national insurance for Year 1.

You also need to pay an Advance payment on account of half of that of £1750 for Year 2.

The total you need to pay in January 2019 is £5250.

This leaves a balance of £3550 in your tax savings account. You deduct a 'bonus' of £1000 for yourself (you've already paid tax on it), keep £1750 for your second Year 2 Advance payment due in July, and keep the other £800 as a 'buffer' incase your earnings (and therefore your future Advance payments) increase this tax year. You continue putting 20% of your income aside each month for tax.

To cut a long story short the two most important things when it comes to Tax are;

Keeping well organised records and receipts

And

Always putting aside a percentage of your income for tax.

Don't treat your income as if 100% of it belongs to you. When you worked for an employer you received your salary with Tax already deducted. If you treat HMRC a bit like an employer you won't have a problem putting aside a percentage of your income ready to pay when it's due, and you definitely won't break the golden rule of not dipping into that money when things are a bit tight.

Remember you haven't paid Tax yet. You will have to pay Tax and that Advance Payment can really put a spanner in the works if you are not prepared.

A final word from HMRC's 'Making Tax Easier' document 2015

"By early 2016, all of the UK's five million small businesses and the first ten million individuals will have access to their own digital tax account. Over time, these will fundamentally transform the way in which taxpayers interact with the tax system.

Taxpayers will get a real-time view of their tax affairs and see how their tax is calculated. They'll also be able to check how much tax they owe or need to be repaid and see their options for paying securely".

Update: The digital tax account is still in the consultation stage but is expected to be in operation for the tax year beginning April 2018 and phased in completely by 2020.

It will mean that:

- You will no longer need to enter information about employment as HMRC will already have it
- Your tax account will operate in 'real time' so you will always know how much tax you owe at any given time
- Because you will update HMRC 4 times a year, the annual return will eventually no longer apply
- Free software and apps will be available to help you manage your digital tax account

Section 2: Tax Allowances and Tax Bands

Tax Allowances

Every year HMRC publish the tax allowances that are available to you. Tax allowances are the amount of money you can earn before you pay tax. The main tax allowance that you need to be aware of is the 'Personal Allowance'. This is the amount of money you are allowed to earn before you start paying any tax. For the year 2017/18 this amount is £11,500. This means you pay tax on everything you earn above that amount. If you earn less than £11,500 then you don't pay any tax.

Once you earn over £100,000 your personal allowance reduces by £1 for every £2 that is you earn above that amount.

If your income is £120,000 you have income that is £20,000 above the £100,000 threshold. £20,000 divided by £2 = £10,000. Your personal allowance reduces by £10,000 therefore you now only have a personal tax allowance of £1000.00.

If you earn £140,000 then your tax allowance reduction would be £20,000, however you personal allowance can only ever reduce to the amount it as set at. So your personal allowance reduces by the 2017/18 rate of £11,500. You would have no personal allowance.

If you earn £105,000 then you are £5000 above the threshold. £5000 divided by £2 = £2500. Your Personal allowance reduces from £11,500 to £9000. You are not taxed on the first £9000 of your income.

Tax Bands

Tax bands are also based on the income that you have. There are three bands, Basic Rate Tax payer, Higher Rate Tax payer and Additional Rate tax payer.

Remember if you earn less than the Personal Tax allowance, currently £11,500, then you do not pay any tax.

If you earn above that amount, but less than an additional £33,500 per year then you are a Basic Rate Tax payer. The current tax rate for a Basic Rate Tax payer is 20% tax.

You earn £35,000 per year. You don't pay tax on the first £11,500; you pay 20% tax on the remaining £23,500.

To remain a Basic Rate Tax payer your income must remain below £45,000 (personal allowance + basic rate tax band amount).

A Higher Rate Tax payer pays a higher rate of tax on everything they earn in the next tax band. The Higher Rate tax band is applied to anything above £33,500 but below £150,000 *after* personal allowance. In real terms, taking into account your personal allowance, this means anything between £45,000 and £150,000.

For income in this band you will pay 40% tax.

You earn £50,000 a year. You don't pay tax on the first £11,500. You pay 20% tax on the next £33,500. You pay 40% on the final £5000.

An Additional Rate Tax payer pays 45% tax on everything they earn above £150,000.

Section 3: National Insurance

People often get confused by the different 'classes' of National Insurance.

Class 1 You pay this if you are employed and your employer deducts it automatically from your salary before you get paid. End of story. There is no cross over between class 1 and any other type of National Insurance. If you are an employee you automatically pay it and how much you pay is a % of your employee pay, not any other income you have.

If you are self employed you could also be paying two other types of national insurance.

Class 4 National Insurance is calculated with your self assessment and paid with your tax every year.

You only pay Class 4 once your self employed income, after expenses, exceeds £8060 for the tax year 2017-18. You pay nothing up to £8164, you pay 9% on everything above that up to £45,000 and then you pay a further 2% on everything above £45,000.

Class 2 National Insurance is also paid on everything you earn above a certain amount. From 2018 Class 2 is being abolished and included in the Class 4 payments system with new thresholds.

However, for 2017-18 the threshold amount is £6025. The rate you pay for the 2017-18 tax year is £2.85 per week. You pay nothing up to £6025, and then you pay £2.80 per week.

HMRC used to send you an invoice for Class 2 regardless of your earnings it is now included in the amount you owe when you complete your self assessment at the end of the tax year.

It's up to you to decide whether you want to either opt out or pay voluntarily if your earnings are less than the threshold.

Payment of Class 2 NI counts towards Incapacity Benefit, the basic State Pension, bereavement benefits and Maternity Allowance.

If you are unsure as to whether to opt out or not, speak to HMRC about your National Insurance credit status as opting out of Class 2 could affect your entitlement to benefits.

If you want to opt out of paying Class 2 National Insurance, because you think you are going to earn less than the threshold for Class 2, you need to contact HMRC and ask for a Class 2 exception. This will mean that HMRC won't expect you to pay Class 2 national insurance.

Section 4: Record Keeping

From an HMRC point of view there are two main ways of record keeping or 'accounting'. You can use the traditional method, called 'Accruals', which is to record every bill you receive and every invoice you issue and pay tax on the difference, even if you haven't paid the bill or received the payment yet.

Or

You can choose to use 'Cash Basis' where you record everything you have actually received and everything you have actually paid and pay tax on the difference. So at the end of the year if you have invoices that have not been paid yet or bills you haven't paid yet they are not included in your total of income and expenses for that year.

Each financial year you can decide which method you want to use, however you can only use 'Cash Basis' if your income (turnover) from your self-employed business/s in a tax year is less that £150,000.

If you exceed this amount in a year you can still carry on using 'Cash Basis' as long as your income doesn't go over £300,000, but then must revert back to using the 'Accruals method' in the next tax year.

You can't use the 'Cash Basis' method if you are a Limited company or a Limited Liability Partnership. The Government introduced this method in April 2013 mainly as a way for the everyday Sole Trader, or Ordinary Partnership to have a simpler way of keeping and understanding their tax records.

There are a number of other business types that can't use the 'Cash Basis' method for example Ministers of Religion. Before you start using it it might be useful to ring HMRC and just check your business type is not excluded.

Record Keeping

One of the main areas where you can fall foul of HMRC is when you don't have proper records of your business.

If you are self employed then the requirements of HMRC are that you keep your records for 5 years after the date when your tax was due. For example, if you finish the year on April 5th 2017, your tax is due by January 31st 2018. You keep your records for that year until 1st February 2021. If HMRC should decide they want to have a look at your accounts and you don't have proper records, you can be fined.

Keeping your records safe

If you keep all your records on a computer, which I do, and you scan copies of receipts rather than keeping paper copies, then you need to make sure you have a secure 'back up' system. The last thing you want to happen is for your computer to crash and to lose all your business records in the process.

I love 'cloud' storage. It's basically a virtual filing cabinet in a secure place on the internet. You have a log in and password and you can store all your records there. It is just like any other folder on your computer and most cloud companies offer a certain amount of free storage that will be more than enough for your one or two person business.

The advantages of cloud storage are that each person can have their own log in, to their own storage, but you can choose to share specific folders with people.

For example you have your virtual filing cabinet (cloud) with four drawers in it (folders). One drawer is for all your personal household information, the other has family photos, the third is for your partnership business and the fourth is for the freelance work you sometimes do on your own.

Your partner also has their own virtual filing cabinet (cloud) with the same cloud company, as does your business partner.

You 'share' the third drawer with your business partner and the first drawer with your partner. You don't share drawer two or four.

Anytime any of you log on to your own cloud you see all your personal folders and you also see your shared folders. You can't see someone else's folders unless they have shared them with you, but the files in the folders will always be the most up to date version of that file.

For example, if your business partner logs on in Basingstoke and updates a document then you log on later in the day in Edinburgh, you see the updated version.

Most clouds also have 'app' versions, so you can use them on your gadgets too. Wherever I go, if I need information I go into the cloud app on my phone or tablet and can immediately access my folders.

A note about security – always have a 6 digit password on any mobile device that you use!!! The last thing you want is to lose your business phone and access to all your information with it. In addition most cloud apps can be set up with an additional password as additional security.

Similarly, on your home laptop or computer, set up a log in and password so that when your kids are on it they are accessing it via their own log in, not yours, and therefore not having access to all your files. This also helps if your equipment ever gets stolen.

Finally, the two greatest things about your virtual filing cabinet are that no matter where you are, as long as you have access to a computer, you can go online and log into your account and access your documents. Great if you are travelling and don't have your laptop etc with you!

And – if your computer crashes – not a problem. Your cloud is still safe and secure, can still be accessed online on an alternative device and all your documents are where they should be. Once your new computer arrives you just download the cloud programme again and off you go!

Section 5: Invoicing

An invoice is a document that you give to each of your customers for any work you do for them. You can invoice at the end of a piece of work, at the end of the month, at the end of the week, it really doesn't matter. Agree with your customer, in advance, when you will invoice them and what your payment terms are (number of days they have to pay your invoice).

If you work for individuals you might decide that payment must be made on demand – they pay you the price you have agreed before you start the job or at the end of the job.

If you work for companies they normally pay you 30 days after you give them your invoice. This can be a bit difficult to manage at the beginning, but as you regularly give customers invoices you will get into a pattern of invoicing and 30 days later receiving payments.

On your invoice you need to include a few standard items:

Name and Address of the business

Invoice number (so you and your customer can track it)

Invoice date

VAT number (if you are registered for VAT)

Supply period (if you are registered for VAT) but can be included anyway if you work for a customer over a time period

Amount owed

VAT (if registered, more about this in the Section on VAT)

Most companies pay their invoices straight into your bank account rather than by cheque, and some will only use this method of payment. It's a good idea to include the following at the bottom of your invoice.

Payment Terms: 30 Days

Please make all payments to YOUR COMPANY NAME/YOUR NAME

Sort Code: XXXXXX   Account Number: XXXXXXXX

If you don't want to design your own invoice, there are lots of invoice templates you can download for free on the web, and Microsoft Word includes many business templates including invoices.

Find out in advance whether your customer is happy to receive emailed invoices and don't be afraid to chase them for payment once those 30 days are up. Get to know the name of the person in the accounts department and if possible get their email. Always be polite, build up a relationship, that way they will be more willing to help you if there is ever a query about your invoice.

You will occasionally be paid late even by big companies. If you provide services to local authorities, educational establishments or companies, late payments are a fact of life. They are normally just due to human error or a break down in the chain of people that authorise your invoice.

This where an overdraft can be useful, if you have one. It can provide the buffer until that late payment comes in, but only if your invoice is guaranteed to be paid! If you have a contract to provide services to large companies or institutions then your late payment is unlikely to be due to a cash flow problem, not necessarily so of the individual or very small company.

Overdrafts shouldn't be used to provide your income whilst you are building up your business; you will never catch up on yourself! Many people that start their own business begin by working as an employee somewhere, as well as being self employed, until they feel confident enough to leap completely into the world of self employment.

What about people who pay in cash, which is more likely of the individual who pays you to fit a light fitting or paint a room…isn't it easy just to ignore that when adding up all your invoices for income purposes?……….HMRC say the following about that…..'*HMRC are closing on undeclared income*'.

It's your decision what you decide to do with that information but if you declare all your income then you have nothing to worry about if HMRC decide they want to inspect your accounts.

Section 6: Expenses

Expenses are all the things you spend money on in the process of 'doing' your business. However, not all of the things you spend money on to do your business are counted as 'allowable expenses' by HMRC. Some expenses have different rules depending on whether you are an employee or self-employed so make sure you are following the correct rule!

Basically, you can spend your money on whatever you want to, but HMRC will only count certain things as money you have spent that can be deducted from your income.

Remember - you make some money, you spend some of the money on things that HMRC sees as valid business expenses, and you pay tax on what is left.

Valid (Allowable) business expenses versus Non-Valid business expenses

HMRC have introduced a flat rate scheme for mileage and for working at home which are explained later in this chapter. You can choose to use both, either, or none regardless of whether you are using the 'Cash Basis' or the 'Accruals' method of accounting discussed in chapter 4.

Clothes

Myth: You can buy yourself a shiny new suit to impress your new customers as you build your business and the cost of the suit can be deducted from your income as a business expense.

Truth: Only safety clothes or clothes with a company logo can be deducted from your income as a business expense. If you need a pair of overall's to paint that room, or a pair of steel toe caps you're fine, but unless that shiny business suit has a logo of your company on the lapel and pocket…its out! You can still buy that suit of course, but it won't make a difference to how HMRC sees your income.

£1000 less £200 for the suit = £1000 income.

£1000 less £200 for the overalls and steel toecaps = £800 income.

Truth: If you are working in certain industries you can claim a flat rate per year as a business expense, if you are responsible for washing your uniform yourself. You can find out what industries here:
http://www.hmrc.gov.uk/manuals/eimanual/eim32712.htm

Working from Home

Working out a 'cost' of using a part of your home for your business can be complex and time consuming. In April 2013 HMRC introduced a flat rate scheme which could save time for the small self-employed person.

Using the flat rate scheme you need to calculate how many average hours a week you work from home running your business. Based on how many hours you spend you calculate your 'home office' cost accordingly in your accounts. Don't forget that the weeks you were on holiday are not weeks you were working from home! Working 'from' home is not the same as working 'at' home. The scheme applies to the time you actually work 'at' home.

The rates from April 2013 onwards are below but be aware that HMRC could change the rates each financial year — make sure you know what the current year rates are each year.

25-50 hours per month: £10 per month

51-100 hours per month: £18 per month

101 hours or more per month: £26 per month

This is not the only method for calculating a 'cost' for working at home but in the ethos of 'SimpleTax' it is the only one that will be covered in this book. HMRC detail the other method on their website if you want to have a look at it.

These monthly amounts are not money you receive from HMRC because you work at home; they are amounts that you deduct as an expense from your profits. Some months you may 25-50 hours a week at home, others 51-100. Keep a notebook next to your computer and write the hours down each day so that you can add it up each month and include the amount in your accounts at the end of the year.

Communications

If you have a dedicated phone line/mobile phone or broadband connection for your business then you simply account for the full cost in your accounts.

If you share your broadband/phone line/mobile phone between business and personal use then you need to work out what percentage is business usage and use that amount in your accounts. One way of doing this is to record usage over a month so that you can get an average percentage for each item. Keep a record of how you made that calculation and keep copies of all your bills relating to these items.

If your communications total £100 a month but 40% of the time they are available for personal use then only £60 is a business cost.

For simplicity and time saving you may prefer to have a mobile phone that is just for business and not bother with a landline, but it depends on what your business requires.

Accommodation and The Business Lunch

Myth: Lunches bought when you are out and about doing your business are allowable business expenses.

Truth: Buying your own lunch is not a business expense. It's a fact of life that you need to eat and HMRC don't see why that means you should pay less tax because of it. There are some exceptions to this.

The first is if you make a journey outside of what you would normally do in your business. So for example, if you normally travel around visiting clients then that is what your business does, but if you have to drive to the other side of the country to collect a piece of machinery then this would be outside your normal daily business and you could claim what HMRC call 'reasonable expenses' for sustenance (lunch etc).

The second exception to this is if you have to spend time overnight, for example for a business trip. If this is the case you can claim for the hotel and reasonable meals. This is not the case if you are based somewhere for a period of time as part of the contract you have been given. HMRC quote overnight as meaning '1 or 2 nights'.

So if you get a contract for 2 weeks work in Portsmouth you can't claim the hotel and food, but if you have to visit Portsmouth and stay for one or two nights then you can. Either way build in the cost of your expenses to complete the contract into your quote.

Myth: Entertaining customers is an allowable expense.

Truth: Taking a client out for lunch is not a business expense even if you are talking about the business.

Professional Fees and other charges

Paying your accountant, business insurance, legal fees in relation to your business are all counted as allowable business expenses.

Paying to advertise your business through advertisement, websites, leaflets and brochures etc are allowable business expenses, as are the costs involved in setting up a website or listing your business in a directory.

If you use a credit card, loan or overdraft to run your business you can include the interest you pay on the amount owed each month. If you are using the 'Cash Basis' method this amount mustn't be more than £500 per year.

Employee Costs

If you decide to have other people in your business, to do some of the work, you will need to decide whether you are sub-contracting them, and they are therefore themselves self-employed, or whether they are employees. It is not a matter of choosing to be either, HMRC have identified a set of distinctive conditions that are a deciding factor in whether the person is your employee or your sub-contractor.

If the worker meets the conditions of an employee then you must follow the rules and procedures relating to PAYE, employee national insurance (Class 1) and employers national insurance. You will also need to ensure that what you decide to pay the worker is at least at the level of the National Minimum wage, and for workers over 25 years old the National Living wage, and that you have taken into account the potential cost of Statutory Maternity, Adoption, Paternity and Sickness pay along with entitlements to annual leave. If your company ceases doing business you will also need to pay Redundancy payments to any worker who has worked for you for at least 2 years.

However, there are financial assistance programmes that you can use to help you with statutory payments for Maternity, Adoption and Paternity leave.

For any worker that you employ who is aged over 22 years and also earns over £10,000 you will need to provide Workplace Pension.

If the worker meets the conditions of a sub contractor or self employed person then you are simply liable for the payment you have agreed to pay them.

The main indicator of whether a worker is employed or self employed is with regard to how much autonomy the person has over the work they do. If they provide their own equipment to complete the work and could, if they wanted to, arrange for someone else to complete the task and can decide when and if they will take on the piece of work then they are probably self-employed. If you can dictate to them what hours they should work and where they should do it and they actually have to do the work themselves then they are probably employed.

It's a good idea to use HMRC's Employment Status Indicator tool for each of your proposed workers. You, and/or they can complete the form online and you could both then could keep a record of the outcome on file.

https://esi2calculator.hmrc.gov.uk/esi/app/index.html

HMRC also have a Helpline for New Employers where you can talk through the details of employing staff.

Administration costs

Everything you buy to do the administration of your business such as postage, specific software, envelopes, printer ink, paper, pens etc is an allowable business expense.

Training courses

Myth: Any training courses you do are an allowable expense.

Truth: Training expenses are only an allowable expense if they relate directly to the business you do. If you are a Plumber and you decide to do a course in a specific area of plumbing to enhance your existing practice then this would probably qualify as an additional expense. If however, you decide you want to be an Electrician as well and go off to get your qualifications to do this; HMRC would probably view this as an additional and new business not part of the existing one. This would not then be an allowable expense.

Carrying forward losses

If you make a loss in your business for a tax year you can 'carry forward' this loss so that it is deducted from your profits in the next tax year. This will then reduce your tax bill for that year.

For example in 2016-17 after all income and allowable expenses your business made a loss of £2000 you would then carry this loss forward to 2017-18.

If in 2017-18 you made a profit of £8000 this would then be actually reduced to £6000 due to the previous year loss. Your tax bill would be calculated against the £6000 not the £8000.

If you made a loss of £1000 in 2016-17 then your new starting balance for 2017-18 would now be minus £3000 as you would have had nothing to reduce the £2000 against due to making a loss again.

Travel Costs

Travel costs, in transport other than your car, for the purpose of doing business are a business expense.

Accounting for the cost of acquiring a Car for business

As a self employed person there are different ways that you can account for the acquiring of a car for business, purchasing a car is covered in the section on Capital Allowances. You could also decide to hire a car on an operating lease or hire a car on a short term rental as and when required.

Operating lease – it's a long term rental where you agree to pay a set amount each month for a set period of time. At the end of the period of time the car is returned with no further payments. You can include the cost of your operating lease in your accounts in full each month less the percentage that you use the car for personal use.

One note of caution – choose a car with CO2 emissions of 130 g/km or less or you will have to deduct 15% of the cost.

If your car is costing £200 a month to lease and it has a CO2 of 160g/km you will only be able to account for £170 a month as a business expense less the percentage for personal use.

The cost of a short term rental works in the same way as an operating lease.

Accounting for the cost of using a car for business

There are two ways you can calculate the cost of using a car.

If you want the simple, no nonsense method, you can use the Flat rate simplified expenses method.

This means for the first 10,000 business miles you drive in a year in a car or van you record an expense of 45p a mile. For every mile over 10,000 you record an expense of 25p a mile. If you use a motorcycle its 24p per mile, regardless of how many you do, and for a bicycle its 20p.

If you carry a business passenger during your journeys you can claim an additional 5p a mile for the part of the journey where they are present.

That's it.

You don't need to keep petrol receipts, receipts for MOT, servicing or anything else to do with your car and you don't have to keep records of your personal mileage. You simply need to keep a record of the journeys you complete every day for your business.

The only additional expense you can claim is the interest part of any loan you have taken out to buy the car or van for the business.

To use the mileage method you need to record the start and end postcodes for each journey and the mileage that you have completed. You can put this onto a spreadsheet each day or week, or you could keep a book in the car that you write in as you go about your daily business. Whatever way you record your journeys, your responsibility is to be able to add up how many miles you have driven for each day/week/month/year and be able to show those records to HMRC if necessary.

Journeys from home to your fixed place of work are not business miles. If you are based at home and you go out to see various customers then the starting place is home.

If you go to a site every day, and then do journeys from there, the journey from home to the site is not a business expense, unless the site is classed as a 'temporary workplace'.

For a site to meet the temporary workplace rule the contractor needs to have an expectation with their customer that they will not be attending the site for more than 24 months. This is called the '24 month rule'. If the contract lasts more, or is even expected to last more than 24 months, even if it doesn't in the end – then it is classed as a permanent place of work and journey expenses cannot be claimed. If the initial agreement is for less than 24 months then the journey's can be claimed.

The exception to this is that the contract may last longer than 24 months but the work involved equates to less than 40% of the contractors normal working time. If this is the case the journeys can be claimed even if the contract lasts longer than 24 months.

A more detailed explanation of this rule can be found here https://www.gov.uk/government/uploads/system/uploads/attachment_data/file/321897/490.pdf

The second way to calculate the cost of using a car is the 'actual' method.

The first thing you need to do with this method is at the start of the financial year record your car milometer. As with the simplified method you record all your business journeys. You also keep receipts for everything you spend on the car e.g. M.O.T, petrol, servicing, tax, insurance.

At the end of the tax year you record your milometer again, calculate how many miles you have done, and what percentage of the total miles are business miles. You then record the same % of the total cost of all your car expenses as a business expense.

Example:

Your start and end milometer shows you have done 8500 miles for the year.

Your total car costs are £5000. Your business miles are 6500 miles. That means 76% of your miles were business miles. 76% of £5000 is £3800. Your allowable business expense for your car is £3800.

The advantage of this method is that you can also include a 'Capital Allowance' for the cost of buying the car or van.

You can only choose one method per car. If you decide that you are using the Mileage method you can't change to the Actuals method until you change your car.

Capital Allowances

Capital Allowances are HMRC's way of dealing with you buying long life (2 years +) equipment, machinery or transportation for your business. It is calculated as a set percentage of the cost of the item and is based on the market value of the item at the date you started using it for your business.

If you buy a car for business use then what you pay is the applicable value. If you decide to start using your existing car for business use then it is based on the value of that car at the point you start using it for business use, not the value of it when you originally bought it.

Capital allowances only apply to the business use percentage of the item. So if you buy a computer for your business but your family use it 50% of the time then only 50% of the allowable capital allowance can be claimed.

A Capital Allowance is not money you receive from HMRC, it is an allowance that is deducted from your profit and therefore reduces the tax you owe.

There are different types of Capital Allowance. The most applicable for a Simple Business are 'Annual Investment Allowance' 'Writing Down Allowance' 'Ist Year Allowance'.

An **Annual Investment Allowance** is a maximum amount that can be offset against your profit each year for the purpose of buying plant and machinery items. Cars cannot be put under this category but Vans can. The Annual Investment amount limit for 1st April 2014 to 31st December 2015 is £500,000. This is a special amount that the government have increased it to motivate growth in the business market; the amount for 1st January 2016 onwards will be £200,000. Again, check each year to ensure it hasn't reduced or increased.

If you buy a Van, a new Computer and a Small forklift truck for your business. All can be calculated within your Annual Investment Allowance. However, each must be individually calculated to take into account any personal use.

Writing Down Allowances can be used in relation to the purchase of cars. For cars with a CO2 of 76g to 130g the Writing Down Allowance is 18%. For cars over 130g it is 8%.

Example:

> You buy a car for £15,000 that has a CO2 of 120g. The writing down allowance of 18% is £2700.
>
> The car is only used 50% of the time for business use so the amount that can be applied to your accounts will be £1350.
>
> You then reduce the cars allowable value for the following year from £15000 to £12300 (£15000-£2700).
>
> The following year you apply 18% of £12300 as your Writing Down Allowance less the percentage for personal use and so on.

First Year Allowances can be used where you have bought a new and unused car for you business with a CO2 of 75g or less. This means you can claim the whole purchase price of the car as an allowance against your profit (less the percentage that is personal use). It can only be used in the year of purchase, rather than for a car you bought in a previous year for personal use, and which was then adopted into your business to be used as a business car in another year.

If you are going to be buying a lot of equipment or machinery for your business speak to a Tax Advisor to ensure you are offsetting the cost against your business in the most effective way.

Section 7: Student Finance and Tax Credits and other benefits

Student finance is calculated yearly for the self employed person. If you are employed and earning above the repayments threshold your employer will automatically deduct student finance from your monthly salary. You will enter the amount that they have already deducted onto your self assessment so that it can be offset against what is due for the year.

If you are completely self employed your self assessment calculation will include an amount for student finance.

Plan 1: If you started your course before 1st September 2012 then for the tax year that starts in April 2017 you will pay 9% of everything you earn above £17,775 per year.

Plan 2: If you started your course after 1st September 2012 you will pay 9% on everything you earn above £21000.

Example:

If you're self employed income is £30000 and you are on plan 1. Your self assessment will include £1100.25 for your yearly student finance payment, to be paid by the 31st January, in addition to the tax, national insurance and advance payment that are due.

If you are on plan 2, with the same income, your payment will be £810.00

Tax Credits are calculated on your income even if that income is self employed income. Claim tax credits in the same way you would if you were employed by an employer. Contact HMRC to discuss your individual situation and working hours so they can give you an indication of what you might be entitled to.

Statutory sick pay is not payable if you are self employed, however if you are unable to work due to illness or disability you may be entitled to Employment Support Allowance.

Maternity Allowance instead of Statutory Maternity Pay is available for self employed people who are expecting a baby It is paid at two rates depending on the amount of time you have been self employed. If you have been employed or self employed earning more than £30 a week for 26 of the previous 66 weeks then you are entitled to the full amount. If you haven't then you are entitled to a reduced amount.

You can find detailed information about Maternity Allowance here https://www.gov.uk/maternity-allowance/overview

Section 8: Self Assessment

Completing the self assessment form is one of those things that a lot of self employed people dread. It all seems so complicated.....right? Wrong, it's actually quite straightforward once you know how to understand the language of HMRC. This section will go through the online self assessment screen by screen, so that when the time comes for you to complete your self assessment you should know *and understand* exactly what you are doing.

SimpleTax doesn't see the point of using the paper version of the self assessment when the online version is easier to understand and calculates everything for you immediately.

The first step in online self assessment is to register for a 'Government Gateway Account'. Once set up this is your online self employed account with HMRC and in it is a record of all the tax you owe and any self assessments or, if applicable, VAT returns you make or have made from the time you set the account up.

If you are newly self employed then you need to register online through HMRC's website. Part of the registration will involve setting up your Government Gateway Account.

If you are already registered for self employed and are still using the paper version of the self assessment form but want to change to the online version you need to set up your Government Gateway Account.

You can set up your Government Gateway Account by going to the web address below. You need to allow plenty of time to do this as it takes a few days for everything to be finalised and accessible.

https://online.hmrc.gov.uk/registration/newbusiness

Once your account is set up and activated you are ready to enter information about your income and expenditure for the year.

You can start your self assessment at any point once the tax year ends on the 5th April. You can choose to enter some of the information and then save it and complete it at another time or you can complete it all at once. You can also finalise and submit the self assessment to HMRC at any time you choose from the 5th April onwards.

The most important thing to remember is that no matter when you complete your self assessment and whether you choose to have it sitting in your account awaiting finalisation before you submit it to HMRC or not – the final date that it must be submitted to HMRC is the 31st January.

If it isn't filed by that date it is 'late' and you will be fined.

The next section will tell you how to complete your self assessment for the current system. Subscribe to the SimpleTax newsletter if you would like further updates.

Information you need to complete your Self Assessment

It will save time and anxiety if, before you start trying to enter anything onto your Self Assessment, you have all the information you need to hand.

-   A print out of your self employed income and allowable expenses for the tax year.

-   Your P60 if, as well as working for yourself, you are also employed by a company for some of the time, or your P45 if you left an employment during the tax year.

-   Information about any profit you received if you are also part of a partnership.

-   Information about any money you received from interest on savings or from income relating to property or oversees investments.

Step by Step completion of Self Assessment

Once you have logged onto your HMRC Gateway Account you have the option to 'file a return'. Once you have clicked on this option you will be taken to the 'Welcome' page. You then need to click on 'Start'.

Section 2 – Tell us about you

Most of this information should be pre-completed. Check that the national insurance number is correct.

The other important box on this page relates to 'Student Loans'. As stated in the chapter on Student Finance, if you have a Student Loan you need to answer this question correctly. If you answer 'no', when it should be 'yes', your self assessment will not calculate how much student finance you owe for the year. If you should have answered yes then HMRC will chase you for the outstanding payment later in the year and possibly fine you for incorrect filing.

You are now ready for the next page. However, after each page you can click on the 'Save' button so that if you decide to finish your return at a later date, all information you have already entered will be saved to your form.

Section 3 – Tailor your return

Section 1: This is the section where your answers will affect which parts of the self assessment form you need to complete. You need to answer yes or no for each of the questions. If you worked for a company as an employee as well as running your own business then you need to say 'yes' to both the employee and self employed boxes. You also need to put the number of companies you were employed by, or the number of businesses you ran, as each one has its own section on the self assessment form.

If you are a Sole Trader running a number of services, such as Tim Smith Gardening, Tim Smith Plumbing and Tim Smith

Kitchen fitting then you are probably classified as running one Sole Trader business not three. However if you are also part of a partnership then its '2'. If you are not sure check with HMRC before you start completing numerous Self Employment pages.

The remaining questions in this section relate to other income – for example, income from UK property income, income from foreign sources e.g. oversees savings and pensions or income from property owned in another country, income from capital gains in this country, Income from interest payments or from pensions. If your income sources are varied and/or complex it's always good to get professional advice as to what needs to be included on the self assessment form.

Section 4: Fill in your return

Completing the sections prior to section 4, tailors your return to suit your individual circumstances. Once you have finished this you are ready to complete the separate sections or 'pages' of the self assessment.

In the Employment page you enter all the details requested, the answers to which can be found on your yearly P60 from your employer.

In the Self Employment pages you begin by ticking any appropriate box that relates to you – for example there are different tax rules for Foster Carers which will impact the information you are asked to provide.

Once you have completed this, the next page will be the basic details of your self employed business. Check these are correct and if you began or ended trading after the beginning or before the end of the current tax year you need to put the applicable dates in this section.

On the next page you need to put the date your accounts are made up to – this is the date your yearly accounts end. For most people this is the same year end date that HMRC use which is the 5th April.

You also need to say Yes or No to whether you are using Cash Basis Accounting (see Section 3).

On the next page you enter your Turnover – the total of all the invoices you have submitted or if using Cash Accounting, the total of all invoices you have been paid.

You then need to enter the total of your allowable expenses. It's quite simple to enter this as a total figure, but you can choose to enter itemised information if you want to. You can enter this figure as the total of all expenses you owe regardless of whether you have paid them all yet, or if using the cash basis system, you will enter only the total of what expenses you have actually paid.

The Net profit is the amount that is liable for tax, less any tax allowances.

Capital allowance amounts are entered on the next page and losses bought forward from previous years (if any) on the page after that.

You then indicate whether you are exempt from Class 4 National Insurance contributions – most people won't be exempt, but you may still not pay anything in the end if you have not met the income threshold.

You have now completed the self employment part of your self assessment.

If you are in a partnership you will now need to complete the partnership pages. Partnerships also have their own unique tax reference number and complete their own separate tax return. The partnership tax return can only be completed by purchasing partnership tax return software, but this is widely available and inexpensive. The profit or loss from the partnership return is split between the partners at whatever percentage you decide. Each partner then enters their individual profit or loss on their own self assessment in the partnership sections.

If your partnership made £5000 profit and you split that 50/50 between two partners, then each partner will enter £2500 as the profit in their individual partnership pages.

If your partnership business has made a loss of £3000 and your share of that is £1500, but your sole trader business has made a profit of £5000, the partnership loss will be included in the total calculation of all your income. In this simple example, that means you have a profit of £3500, not £5000, due to the £1500 partnership loss.

Section 5: If you have received any other UK income you need to enter it on the following pages.

You have now completed all your income pages including, if applicable, those relating to interest, pensions and capital gains.

The next part of the self assessment relates to underpaid or over paid tax from previous years and any student loan repayments that you may have had deducted by an employer you work for.

Answer the questions about any overpaid or underpaid tax from previous years and then enter the total amount of any student finance deductions from any employment pay made in the current tax year.

If you owe a small amount of tax, and also work for an employer, you have the option of having the tax collected monthly via your PAYE deductions instead of paying HMRC directly yourself. You need to indicate on your tax return whether or not you would like this to happen.

Once you have completed the sections on your self assessment you will be at the 'Check your return' page. On this page you will see a list of all the sections you needed to complete and either a tick or a cross next to each section. Any crosses mean there are parts of the self assessment that are not complete. You can click on any incomplete parts to add information. Once the self assessment is complete every section will have a tick next to it.

To sum up, with regard to self assessment, you can be employed, self-employed, a Partner in an Ordinary or Limited liability partnership, receive foreign or UK property income and interest from savings or any or all of the above. When you 'tick' the boxes that apply in the 'Tailor your return' section it will automatically generate only the pages you need to complete.

Section 6: View your calculation

This section shows a summary of how much, in total, tax, national insurance, and if applicable student loan payments, are due by the 31st January. It does not include any payments on account you have already paid. It also shows the amounts you need to pay as Advance Payments on 31st January and 31st July.

On this page you can "view and print your calculation". It's a good idea to view and either save or print the calculation before you move on. Viewing your calculation will show you the full breakdown of all your types of income, your tax allowance, your total expenses, national insurance and student finance due and the deduction for any student finance or tax already paid via PAYE.

Once you click to the next page you will be asked if you want to reduce your Advance Payments. If you say 'yes', because you think your current years income is going to be yes than what you earned in the year ending, you can reduce your payments accordingly. However, if you reduce your payments and then it turns out you should have paid more because your income was in fact comparable with the year just ended, you will be charged interest on the difference between the amount you should have paid and the amount you actually paid.

You are now ready to <u>Save your tax return</u> and <u>Submit your tax return.</u>

At any point up until the 31st January you can return to your tax return and make an amendment. Making amendments after this point is allowable and you can do so online up to 12 months after the tax deadline of 31st January. If you need to make amendments after this time period has passed you will need to contact HMRC directly to do so.

Section 9: Fines and Penalties

Late Filing of Self Assessment

Late filing of self assessment can be very costly and HMRC
will chase fines and tax due and use debt collection if
necessary

Missing the filing deadline	£100.00
3 months late	Daily penalty of £10 per day for up to 90 days
6 months late	A further 5% of tax due or £300
12 months late	A further 5% of tax due or £300

Interest on Late payment of tax due

30 days late	5% of tax due
6 months late	5% of tax outstanding
12 months late	5% of tax outstanding

Advance Payments

Late payment penalties are not charged on Advance
Payments, but interest is. Just because your Advance

payment relates to tax not technically due until 31st January doesn't mean HMRC wont' chase you for it.

If you can't afford to make your Advance Payment on the 31st January and the 31st July you need to contact HMRC to make an arrangement with them.

Even though the tax for the year that has just ended isn't technically due until 31 January the following year, HMRC are hot on chasing up advance payments and they may use debt collectors if you haven't paid it on time and haven't made an arrangement with them to pay it.

Example:

If in January 2017 you pay £5000 tax for the year 2015-16, you will also need to pay £5000 as an estimate of tax that will be due in January 2018 for tax year 2016-17.

To pay this £5000 you will pay £2500 on 31st January 2017 and £2500 in July 2017. That is why it is so important to put away that 20% of your income right from the very first month you become self-employed. If you do that then Advance Payments won't scare you.

Tax Inspections

In theory, HMRC target some businesses if they suspect that tax fraud is taking place, however they also choose businesses randomly to check accounts and records.

HMRC will write or telephone you and inform you that they wish to check your accounts and ask to see certain information. For the business that has kept accurate records for the timescales specified this should be no problem. They will give you a timescale to provide the information and it may be that you will be asked to post it into them or to meet a representative at your nearest tax office. If the meeting is to take place in person you can take your accountant or someone else such as a relative with you to support you during the meeting.

If you don't provide the information in the timescale provided HMRC may fine you. The fine could be any of the following, £300.00, or up to £60.00 per day or a percentage of tax they believe you owe them.

However, if the delay is due to a serious illness or death of a relative HMRC will discuss delaying the submission date with you.

Once HMRC have assessed all the information they have asked for they will write to you with their decision about their inspections. This may mean they agree your accounts are correct, they may inform you of an error you have made which will result in you owing more tax, or they may inform you of an error meaning you have paid too much tax and are therefore due to receive a refund possibly with interest.

If you have made an error resulting in you not paying enough tax then you may receive a fine. The amount of the fine will be based on whether they believe the underpayment was due to a mistake or a deliberate intention to underpay tax.

Section 10: Value Added Tax

Value Added Tax otherwise known at VAT is often something that seems a bit mysterious. It's actually fairly straightforward for the simple self employed business. However, be warned, the VAT office have far reaching powers to reclaim VAT that they are owed. VAT registration requires discipline and diligence at all times.

It is mandatory for businesses with a turnover (all the money you receive) of £85000 or over in a tax year to register for VAT.

Businesses that have a turnover of less than £85,000 (2017/18) can choose to register for VAT voluntarily and it could be financially beneficial to do so. The rest of this section focuses only on those who can choose whether to register or not, not on those who have to register because their turnover is £85,000 or higher.

If your business mainly supplies to companies or organisations, who are themselves VAT registered, then registering for VAT could be useful in increasing the money in your pocket at the end of the tax year.

Companies who are registered for VAT are not concerned if you are registered and charge for VAT as they can use one of the VAT schemes to reclaim the VAT they pay you.

If however, most of your clients are people. You may decide VAT registration isn't for you as it will increase what you charge for your services. For example if you are a painter and decorator who charges VAT but your nearest competitor doesn't, then the householder obtaining the quotes may choose the competitor rather than you, as they are not able to reclaim the VAT they pay you.

Once you register for VAT you have to charge VAT on all of your services. You cannot choose to charge VAT to one customer but not another. However, you can decide to de-register for VAT at any time too. So if half way through the year you find VAT registration is not beneficial you then deregister and only pay VAT owed up to that point.

How does VAT work?

You charge VAT on your services at the rate specified by the government – currently 20%. You calculate how much VAT you have paid and deduct that from what you have charged and pay the HMRC the rest.

VAT is paid to HMRC quarterly. The long winded way of calculating how much VAT you owe is to keep every receipt for everything you spend in your business for the quarter (which is why petrol stations always ask if you want a VAT receipt). You then need to add up all the VAT you have spent and deduct it from what you have charged for the quarter, you owe HMRC the difference.

If your business mainly supplies to companies or organisations who are themselves VAT registered <u>and</u> your business doesn't involve buying lots of stock, or lots of customers that invoice you for VAT, then registering for VAT <u>and also</u> the VAT flat rate scheme is a much simpler method of calculating your VAT repayment.

Using the flat rate scheme means you won't have to keep a record of all the VAT you paid and all the VAT you charged. You will simply pay a percentage of your invoices to HMRC each quarter. This can be advantageous if you don't have a lot of VAT purchases. You can still in addition reclaim the VAT on any Capital Goods that you buy for your business as long as the purchase is in excess of £2000 including VAT.

How does the flat rate scheme work?

You add up all your invoices for the quarter and pay HMRC a flat rate percentage. This means you don't have to keep a record of all the VAT you have paid when paying for petrol and other expenses.

The flat rate percentage is decided by HMRC dependent on what business sector you are in. For example, currently, the percentage for Social Work is 11% and for Computer repair services its 10.5% and so on.

The flat rate percentages can be found here.

http://www.hmrc.gov.uk/vat/start/schemes/flat-rate.htm#2

It may be that you do more than one kind of business. HMRC expect you to apply the flat rate that applies to the part of your business that generates the most money, and then use this rate for the other parts of your business too. They do not want you to use different rates for different things. The flat rate scheme is supposed to make VAT simple not over complicate it. You should review this every year as it may be that one part of your business starts to be more profitable than another and the rate will need to change for the New

Year. This should be the year according to when you registered for VAT not the financial year. So if you register for VAT on the 1st July, you should review your business sectors on the 1st July the following year and make any necessary changes to the flat rate percentage you are using.

HMRC have made it even more attractive by applying a first year discount of 1% discount on the published flat rate percentage. So if your flat rate is 11%, for the first year you only pay 10%.

There is however one fly in the ointment! **From the 1st April 2017** the flat rate scheme is changing. If your business spends 2%, and this must equate to at least a £1000 a year, on what HMRC classes as 'goods' then you will be able to use the flat rate scheme percentage for your business sector as usual.

If you spend less than this then you will be classed as a 'limited costs business'. You will have to use the new flat rate % of 16.5%, when you register for the flat rate scheme, regardless of your business sector although the 1% first year discount still applies.

There are quite a few categories of expenditure that will not count as 'goods' such as fuel unless you are a transport company. A comprehensive list can be found in section 4.6 of HMRC's guidance.

https://www.gov.uk/government/publications/vat-notice-733-flat-rate-scheme-for-small-businesses/vat-notice-733-flat-rate-scheme-for-small-businesses#para4-4

What this all means is that, due to the new rules, if you mainly provide services rather than goods you may find it is not as beneficial to register for VAT/flat rate scheme as it once was.

What does it actually mean in practice if you decide to join the flat rate scheme?

In April, May and June you charge £1000 per month to your customer. Your flat rate for VAT is 11% but you have a first year discount of 1%.

£1000 + (20%) VAT = £1200

For the quarter, including VAT, your invoice total is £3600. With the first year discount you need to pay 10% as flat rate VAT. You owe HMRC £360.00.

If you didn't charge VAT you would have earned £3000.

By charging VAT, even after paying HMRC your flat rate, you have still earned £3240 for the quarter.

You have £240 more in your pocket for the quarter than if you hadn't' charged VAT.

You will still pay tax on ALL your profit including the money you 'make' on VAT.

So using the very simple example above, and not taking into account national insurance thresholds or personal allowances, if your profit at the end of the year is £12960 (4 X £3240) and you paid 20% tax and 9% National Insurance you will still have approximately £9200 in your pocket compared to £8500 if you hadn't charged VAT.

What do you charge VAT on?

VAT must be charged on everything you charge your customer except 'disbursements'.

A 'disbursement' is a direct client cost that you pay with permission of and on behalf of your customer. In my business I rent a venue and provide refreshments for clients who have been referred to me by my customer. I invoice my customer for the exact amount I am charged for providing this. It is the customer's responsibility to ensure that a venue and refreshments are provided; I am therefore acting on their behalf.

HMRC expect you to show the total of disbursements separately on your invoice and VAT should not be charged on them.

'Everything else' means anything else you charge your customer in respect of your agreement to provide a service to them. For example, if as part of that agreement they have agreed to pay your travel costs, either mileage or other travel costs, VAT must be charged on those costs.

This can seem confusing as often on receipts you will see an amount for VAT has already been made by the supplier so it can seem like VAT is being charged twice. HMRC are not interested in how the receipt is broken down, they are only interested in what you charged the customer (the total cost of the item) and that you charged VAT on it. If you paid £50 for travel expenses, but decided to only charge the customer 50% of those costs that's up to you, but you must charge VAT on whatever amount you charge your customer.

What information needs to be provided to HMRC?

First you need to register online for VAT. This is done through your Government Gateway Account. Once logged into your account you can 'Enrol for service'. You will receive a confirmation email within a few days stating that you are enrolled. You will also receive a letter confirming your VAT number. This number must be quoted on every invoice.

You also need to register for the Flat Rate scheme. You can do this online when you register for VAT or by completing the form at the link below and posting it to HMRC.

http://www.hmrc.gov.uk/forms/vat600frs.pdf

If the two applications are made close together then you can start the flat rate from the date that you register for VAT.

You then need to complete the online VAT return every quarter. When you enrol for VAT HMRC will tell you which months your VAT return is due. You can also sign up email alerts. This means HMRC will email you near the month end to remind you that your VAT return is due.

Once your VAT return is completed, the VAT you owe will be paid to HMRC by direct debit approximately 6 weeks later. Once you submit your VAT return you will receive an online message stating which date your payment will come out of your account.

All you need to do is to remember that just because all that VAT is sitting in your account – doesn't mean it's all yours.

You haven't paid VAT to HMRC yet, you will have to pay VAT to HMRC.

Just like with your taxes, organisation and discipline are key.

Completing the online VAT return for the Flat Rate Scheme

In order to complete the online VAT return for the Flat Rate scheme you need a few figures from your accounts.

You need to calculate the % you owe to HMRC. So if your total is £5000 and your flat rate percentage is 10% then this figure is £500.00. This is called Output Tax.

This amount goes in Box 1 of the Online VAT return.

You need to know the total amount you have invoiced in the VAT period you are doing the return for. The figure needs to include the VAT you have charged. This is called Input Tax. So if you have invoiced £4166.66 + 20% VAT (£833.33), your total Input tax is £5000, not £4166.66.

This amount goes in Box 6 of the Online VAT return.

If you are reclaiming the VAT you have paid on a Capital Purchase you need to enter the amount of VAT you are reclaiming in Box 4 of the Online VAT return.

If you are using the 'cash accounting' method you only include the figures for money you have actually received at the point of the return.

Therefore, if you are doing a vat return for April May and June on the 30th June, and you have invoiced £5000 per month including VAT but have only been paid for April and May and not yet received the June amount, then your total input Tax is £10,000 and your Output tax is based on that. You will pay the remaining output tax on the June amount on your next VAT return (if you have been paid it by then).

You can find a more detailed explanation of how to complete your VAT return by using the link below.

http://customs.hmrc.gov.uk/channelsPortalWebApp/channel sPortalWebApp.portal?_nfpb=true&_pageLabel=pageImport _ShowContent&id=HMCE_CL_000345&propertyType=docum ent#P331_29331

Conclusion

This book was always intended to be a no nonsense beginner's guide to Tax and Accounts in plain English for the simple self employed business. Hopefully it has met its intention of giving you the information you need to spend less time pouring over receipts and invoices and more time doing what you like doing best – running your business.

No book can cover every aspect of Tax, which can be a complex system, but hopefully everything you need to run that simple one or two person business is included here. I would always encourage you to seek advice from the many sources that are available, books, internet, HMRC webinairs, tax advisors. The more information you have the more in control you will be of your self employed business.

Maybe you are just beginning your self employed journey and haven't had a clue how to begin when it comes to Tax, or maybe you have been self employed for years but still feel that you don't have the information you need to manage your self employed business. Hopefully the information in this book with give you the head start you need as you become more and more brilliant at what you do!

If you would like to sign up for tax tips and updates please register on the website.

Glossary

HMRC = Her Majesty's Revenue and Customs, the department responsible for collecting tax

Revenue = all the money you receive from 'doing' your self employed work

Business expenses = the money you spend 'doing' your self employed work

Turnover = all the money you earn in a tax year

Profit = Turnover minus Expenses

Taxable income = the amount of money you will pay tax on (the same as profit)

Tax Allowance = the amount of money you can earn before you pay any tax (2017-18 = £11500)

The Tax Year = HMRC's tax year starts on the 6th April and ends on the 5th of April the following year

Payment of Tax = the payment you make for all tax due for the tax year. It must be paid by the 31st January following the end of the tax year

Self- Assessment = the document you complete to show HMRC your Turn over and your business expenses so that they the calculation can be made as to how much tax you need to pay on your taxable income

Registering as Self Employed = you must tell HMRC within 3 months of starting your self employed work

Student loan = if you owe student finance for your student loan, the yearly payment will be calculated when you complete your self assessment form and the payment for the year will need to be paid in full along with the tax you owe

Payment in advance = the amount you will pay on 31st January and 31st July for payments that will be due on the following 31st January.

Late payment penalties = Penalties that HMRC charge if you do not pay tax by the due date (31st January). Late payment penalties are not charged on advanced payments

Maternity Allowance = A weekly amount you may be entitled to if you are self employed and expecting a baby

Employment Support Allowance = A weekly amount you may be entitled to if you are self employed and unable to work due to sickness or ill health

Capital Allowances = Amounts you include in your accounts for machinery/cars/vans etc that you buy for your business that reduce your tax bill

VAT = value added tax. A charge of 20% that you add to your invoices once registered for VAT

Sole Trader = a single person trading

Ordinary Partnership = Two or more people trading together

A Limited Liablity Partnership = Two or more people trading together where the individual partners have some protection about debts incurred by the partnership or the conduct of individual partners should that prove to be fraudulent etc.

References

Tax Credit Helpline: 0345 300 3900

Employers Helpline: 0300 200 3200

Self Assessment Helpline: 0300 200 3310

VAT Helpline: 0300 200 3700

https://www.gov.uk/government/uploads/system/uploads/attachment_data/file/413975/making-tax-easier.pdf

Cash accounting

https://www.gov.uk/simpler-income-tax-cash-basis

VAT

http://customs.hmrc.gov.uk/channelsPortalWebApp/channelsPortalWebApp.portal?_nfpb=true&_pageLabel=pageLibrary_PublicNoticesAndInfoSheets&propertyType=document&columns=1&id=HMCE_CL_000345#P35_2315

Disbursements

http://www.hmrc.gov.uk/vat/managing/charging/disbursements.htm

http://www.hmrc.gov.uk/manuals/bimmanual/Index.htm

Simplified Accounts and Cash basis – HMRC

https://www.youtube.com/watch?v=CmU2EbUNgiQ&list=PLD4760DD51E2F0045&index=23

The Business Lunch

http://www.hmrc.gov.uk/manuals/bimmanual/bim37670.htm

Tax Inspections

https://www.gov.uk/self-assessment-tax-return-checks

Hmrc Webinair   http://www.hmrc.gov.uk/webinars/

About the Author

Denice Houslin wanted to run her own business for as long as she can remember. She has successfully done so since 2010, providing conflict resolution and family group work in social care. On her journey of self employment Denice was often asked for advice on tax matters by others in her teams. Thus began a passion for being able to explain tax in a way that the everyday person 'doing' their self employed business could understand. Alongside her writing, Denice also provides One to One and Group Coaching and Mentoring services on 'Simple Tax' for the self employed.

Denice has a degree in Psychology and qualifications in Mediation, Counselling and Coaching and is currently studying for her Tax Advisor qualification

https://twitter.com/simpletaxuk

https://www.facebook.com/simpletaxuk

www.simpletaxuk.co.uk

Disclaimer

30170874R00042

Printed in Great Britain
by Amazon